Truth
AND
Authority
IN
Modernity

Christian Mission and Modern Culture

EDITED BY
ALAN NEELY, H. WAYNE PIPKIN,
AND WILBERT R. SHENK

In the series:

Believing in the Future, by David J. Bosch

Write the Vision, by Wilbert R. Shenk

Truth and Authority in Modernity,
by Lesslie Newbigin

Religion and the Variety of Culture,
by Lamin Sanneh

Truth
AND
Authority
IN
Modernity

LESSLIE NEWBIGIN

TRINITY PRESS INTERNATIONAL
Valley Forge, Pennsylvania

Gracewing.

This book is a revision and expansion of an essay published in *Faith and Modernity*, edited by Philip Samson, Vinay Samuel and Chris Sugden (Oxford: Regnum/Lynx Books, 1994), and in *A Word in Season*, edited by Eleanor Jackson (Grand Rapids: Wm. B. Eerdmans, 1994), and used herewith by permission.

First published by
TRINITY PRESS INTERNATIONAL
P.O. Box 851
Valley Forge, PA 19482-0851
U.S.A.

First British edition
published by
GRACEWING
2 Southern Avenue
Leominster
Herefordshire HR6 0QF
England

Trinity Press International is part of the Morehouse Publishing Group.

Cover design: Brian Preuss

Library of Congress Cataloging-in-Publication Data

Newbigin, Lesslie.
    Truth and authority in modernity / Lesslie Newbigin. – 1st U.S. ed.
        p.   cm. – (Christian mission and modern culture)
    Includes bibliographical references (p.   ).
    ISBN 1-56338-168-0 (pbk. : alk. paper)
    1. Authority–Religious aspects–Christianity. 2. Truth (Christian theology) 3. Mission of the church. 4. Christianity and culture. 5. Civilization. Modern–20th century. 6. Postmodernism–Religious aspects–Christianity. I. Title. II. Series.
BT88.N36   1996
231'.042–dc20   96-13846
                                                                              CIP

Gracewing ISBN 0-85244-377-3

Printed in the United States of America

96   97   98   99   00   01   6   5   4   3   2   1

Contents

Preface to the Series

Both Christian mission and modern culture, widely regarded as antagonists, are in crisis. The emergence of the modern mission movement in the early nineteenth century cannot be understood apart from the rise of technocratic society. Now, at the end of the twentieth century, both modern culture and Christian mission face an uncertain future.

One of the developments integral to modernity was the way the role of religion in culture was redefined. Whereas religion had played an authoritative role in the culture of Christendom, modern culture was highly critical of religion and increasingly secular in its assumptions. A sustained effort was made to banish religion to the backwaters of modern culture.

The decade of the 1980s witnessed further momentous developments on the geopolitical front with the collapse of communism. In the aftermath of the breakup of the system of power blocs that dominated international relations for a generation, it is clear that religion has survived even if its institutionalization has undergone deep change and its future forms are unclear. Secularism continues to oppose religion, while technology has emerged as a major source of power and authority in modern culture. Both confront Christian faith with fundamental questions.

The purpose of this series is to probe these developments from a variety of angles with a view to helping the church understand its missional responsibility to a culture in crisis. One important resource is the church's experience of two centuries of cross-cultural mission that has reshaped the church into a global Christian *ecumene*. The focus of our inquiry will be the church in modern culture. The series (1) examines modern/postmodern culture from a missional point of view; (2) develops the theological agenda that the church in modern culture must address in order to recover its own integrity; and (3) tests fresh conceptualizations of the nature and mission of the church as it engages modern culture. In other words, these volumes are intended to be a forum where conventional assumptions can be challenged and alternative formulations explored.

This series is a project authorized by the Institute of Mennonite Studies, research agency of the Associated Mennonite Biblical Seminary, and supported by a generous grant from the Pew Charitable Trusts.

Editorial Committee

ALAN NEELY

H. WAYNE PIPKIN

WILBERT R. SHENK

1

Divine Authority

If the reality that we seek to explore, and of which we are a part, is the work of a personal Creator, then authority resides in this one who is the Author. If, on the other hand, this reality is the result of processes within itself — if, for example, it is the outcome of a struggle for existence in which the strongest survives the rest — then authority is simply one way of describing superior strength. Power and authority are one and the same. The Christian tradition maintains, of course, that the former is the case, that authority resides in the One who is the Author of all being. And because personal being can be known only insofar as the person chooses to reveal herself or himself, and cannot be known by the methods that are appropriate to the investigation of impersonal matters and processes, then authority, in this view, must rest on divine revelation. Modernity has declined to accept this authority.

In the opening chapters of Matthew's Gospel, Jesus is heard teaching the people of Israel with the formula: "You have heard that it was said to them of former times.... But I say to you...." Not surprisingly we then read that his hearers were astonished, because he taught as one having authority, and not as their scribes. Immediately thereafter we see Jesus healing a leper with a single authoritative word. The teaching of the scribes rested on the authority of the Torah. Jesus taught as one who had no need of such reference; he himself embodied final authority. Here is the point at which Christian teaching about authority finally rests. There have been and still are sharp disagreements among Christians about the way in which this authority is mediated to the present life of the Christian community. These will be discussed in the second part of this volume. For the present I will be concerned with modernity's rejection of this central claim.

Modernity's Suspicion of Authority

For the purpose of this volume I am assuming
that in speaking of "modernity" we are speaking
about the way of thinking that came to dominance in the intellectual leadership of Europe —
though with roots running far back into the
past — a way of thinking that rejected appeals to
revelation and tradition as sources of authority
except insofar as they could justify themselves
before the bar of individual reason and conscience. Reliable, and therefore authoritative,
knowledge of truth is not, in the view of modernity, to be found by faith in alleged revelation,
but by observation of the facts and rigorously
critical reflection on them. Typical of modernity
is John Locke's definition of faith: "a persuasion
of our own minds short of knowledge" (cited
by Polanyi 1958, 266). This may be contrasted
with the famous slogan of Augustine: *credo ut
intelligam;* I believe in order that I may know.
Here faith is understood not as an alternative
to knowledge but as the pathway to knowledge.
We do not come to know anything except by
believing something. We have to begin by believing the evidence of our senses, the veracity
of our teachers, and the validity of the tradition

into which we are seeking apprenticeship. All of
these things may have to be questioned at some
stage, but we can question them only on the basis of things that we have come to know as the
result of this kind of apprenticeship. We do not
begin to acquire any kind of knowledge by laying
down in advance the conditions upon which we
will accept any evidence. We have to begin with
an openness to a reality greater than ourselves in
relation to which we are not judges but pupils.

But throughout the history of European
Christianity there has always been another
powerful element deriving from the tradition of
Greek rationalism. This achieved a great impetus
through the translation into Latin, during the
tenth and eleventh centuries, of the great Islamic
commentaries on Aristotle. As is well known,
the impact of this on the thought of Western
Europe was immense. It led to the creation of
the universities and the rise of "the new science."
What is important from the point of view of the
present discussion is that it also led to the great
work of Thomas Aquinas in which he restated
the Christian tradition in the light of the new
intellectual situation. Part of this restatement involved a distinction between those things that
can be known by the work of reason alone and

those things that can be known only by revelation
and faith. Among the former were included the
knowledge of the existence of God and of the
soul; among the latter, such things as the Trinity,
the Incarnation, and the Atonement. It is hard
to exaggerate the influence of this on all later
thinking in the western church. The Jesuit theo-
logian Michael Buckley (1987) sees this as the
point at which modern atheism had its origins.
The arguments for the existence of God are always fragile. Buckley argues that a fatal step was
taken when the church called in the help of "The
Philosopher," as Aristotle was so often called, to
provide an assurance for faith, rather than relying for its assurance upon that which was given
in Jesus Christ.

The results of this fatal step became very
apparent during the profound disturbance of
thought that resulted from the radically new
cosmology opened by the work of Galileo,
Copernicus, and Kepler. It seemed that all the
assured certainties were being overturned. How
could one be sure of God, of the soul, or of
anything else? It was in this climate of extreme
uncertainty and skepticism that René Descartes
received a commission from a cardinal of the
Roman Catholic Church to develop a certain

proof of the existence of God and of the soul. We are familiar with the way in which he responded to this commission, finding certainty in the existence of his own thinking mind and seeking to build on this with logical arguments that had the clarity and the indubitability of mathematics. I am not concerned here with these arguments but with the entire enterprise. What are we to make of this demand for a proof of the existence of God that assumes that there are grounds more trustworthy than those given in God's own self-revelation? If God really exists, is there not something ridiculous about one of God's creatures taking a stance that, in effect, says to God: "I can demonstrate your existence without relying on what you tell me about yourself." And (once again, if God really exists), is it not even more absurd for this creature to regard his own alleged proofs as the necessary basis for his attention to the divine revelation? Yet how otherwise can we regard the long tradition of natural theology seen as the necessary prolegomena for the study of God's self-revelation in Christ as witnessed in Scripture?

It is now clear that Descartes' method, which has dominated subsequent European thought, has in it the seeds of its own destruction. The corollary of that method was the famous "critical principle." Reliable knowledge is that which can be achieved by starting from indubitable certainties and building on them arguments that have the clarity and indubitability of mathematics. Reliable knowledge, for which the word *science* is henceforth used, has mathematics as its working language. What falls outside the scope of this certain knowledge is to be doubted. All claims to knowledge must pass through the fire of critical questioning so that claims to knowledge that are based merely on faith are to be distinguished from knowledge that can be certainly proved. Augustine's maxim is therefore reversed. The pathway to knowledge is not faith but doubt. "Honest doubt" is contrasted with "blind faith" in the folk language of modernity.

The Postmodern Reaction

The Cartesian program proves to be inherently self-destructive for the simple reason that doubt, if it is to be rational, must rest upon something that is believed to be true. If I say, "I doubt the proposition P," and am asked for my reasons, I will have to reply in one of two ways. Either

I must say, "Because I believe Q, and Q is not compatible with P," or else, "Because P has not been proved"; and the latter assertion implies my belief that there are grounds on which P could be shown to be either true or false. In both cases my doubt is rational only if these beliefs are in place. Plainly, both faith and doubt have necessary roles in the enterprise of knowing; but the role of doubt, necessary as it is, is secondary, and that of faith primary. We can know without doubting, but we cannot know without believing. The Cartesian invitation to make doubt the primary tool in the search for knowledge was bound to lead to the triumph of skepticism and eventually of nihilism, as Nietzsche foresaw. The demand for a kind of indubitable certainty that does not depend on faith has led inexorably to despair about the possibility of knowing anything. We are in the situation that Nietzsche anticipated where rational argument ceases and the only arbiter is power and the will to power. Even science, the glory of our modern European society and still the most dynamic element in it, is no longer seen as a pathway to wisdom, to a true understanding of the human situation; rather, it is seen as a means to power. The vastly greater part of all scientific work is now devoted to the search for power — military, industrial, commercial. If one looks at the characteristic products of contemporary European society in the areas of literature, drama, art, and music, the picture is one of nihilism. Claims to know and speak truth are regarded merely as claims to dominance on the part of that section of society from which they emerge. There are successive "regimes of truth" (Foucault) that succeed one another, each one repressing rival claims by the use of force until overturned by the next. There is no truth beyond this. The corollary on the personal level is narcissism, an obsession with the self, its development and its internal history.

There is profound irony in this story: the relapse into nihilism and narcissism is the end product of the search for indubitable knowledge as distinct from the knowledge that is claimed to be available through faith in the divine revelation. Yet for those standing in the biblical and Christian tradition, this story should not be surprising. If it is really the case that God is the author of all being, including our own, then all claims to knowledge starting from elsewhere must end in confusion. The search for an authority prior to and more basic than the authority of God's self-revelation must end in failure. This statement has, of course, immediate implications for what is called natural theology, but its implications are far wider and cover the whole range of human knowing. R. A. Clouser (1991), in his book *The Myth of Religious Neutrality,* has shown convincingly how the great scientific theories take as their starting point some belief about what is ultimate and fundamental in the area of their study. In other words, they start from a belief about what religious people call "god." And, by definition, the starting point cannot be validated by any kind of a priori proof. It can be validated only, if at all, by its fruitfulness. And if it is true that the ultimate and fundamental reality is God as he has made himself known in the history that has Jesus Christ as its center, then theories that take some other starting point and that claim to give a comprehensive interpretation of the cosmos must end in illusion. The biblical statement that "the fear of the Lord is the beginning of wisdom" has a much wider range of importance than is commonly recognized. If fully understood, in fact, this small sentence would be seen to be subversive of the central thrust of modernity.

Authority: External and Internal

Modernity is distrustful of authority. It was born in a movement of emancipation from what were seen as external authorities, and its appeal was to the freedom and responsibility of the individual reason and conscience to judge between rival claims to truth. In the famous words of Kant, its slogan has been "Dare to know." And there are many situations in which this is the most important thing to say. Authority that is merely imposed from outside is not true authority. We are so made that we need to see for ourselves that something is true or right. Yet, if this demand for individual freedom of judgment is taken as our sole guide to reality, we are in trouble. There is a story about a visitor to the Uffizzi gallery in Florence who came out and said, "I don't think much of the stuff here," to which the janitor replied, "It is not the pictures but the visitors who are on trial here." Even as we claim freedom of judgment, we must know that in judging we are judged. There is another story of a visitor who went round a gallery with a guidebook in which the works exhibited were shown with one, two, or three asterisks in accordance with their distinction as works of art. After looking at each picture and then at the text of the guidebook, the visitor was heard to murmur: "good," "lovely," or "marvelous," in accordance with the indications given by the book. Even though we know that we are judged in our judging, there is no escape from the responsibility for making personal judgment. But my personal judgment must be provisional, tempered by the recognition that I have more to learn. My judgment is not the last word. I have to be open to things that I have not yet understood. In this sense authority has to be external; it refers to a reality beyond myself. But, if it is to be authoritative for me, I must come to the point of recognizing its authority. It has to be internalized.

The implications of this would seem to be that the proper human relation to the reality with which we have to do is that of a learner, an apprentice. All our knowing comes to us through our apprenticeship in a tradition of knowing that has been formed through the effort of previous generations. This tradition is the source of the mental faculties through which we begin to make sense of the world. In this sense the tradition has authority, but it is not a purely external authority. We are responsible for internalizing the tradition by our struggle to understand the world with the help of the tools it furnishes, and in this process the tradition itself develops and is changed. This calls for a combination of reverence for the tradition with courage to bring our own judgment to bear upon its application to new circumstances. The idea that we could construct an entire edifice of knowledge without reliance on the tradition by the exercise of our own powers of observation and reasoning (an idea that was certainly present in the formative process of modernity) is surely illusion. We are not in a position where we could lay down in advance the terms on which we will accept any claim to truth.

By Grace Alone

What are the implications of saying that authority must be both external and internal? If we are thinking not of secular knowledge but of the knowledge of God and of the recognition of the authority of God, does it lead to a sort of Pelagianism? Does it mean that God is not sovereign because we have to contribute our part to the recognition of his authority? Do we have to speak not only of divine revelation but also of a human "capacity for revelation," without which divine revelation would be ineffectual?

We are here in the midst of the battlefield in which Barth and Brunner waged their famous battle in the 1930s. For many people, at least in the Anglo-Saxon world, it seemed that Brunner's was the reasonable position and that Barth's angry "NO" was irrational. For Barth it was a matter of life and death to affirm that faith itself, the capacity to recognize and receive God's revelation, is God's gift and not a human achievement. This was something that struck at the very heart of modernity. It seemed to be a direct assault on human freedom and responsibility.

To grasp the issues here, we must take account of a dimension of the human situation that the argument hitherto has ignored. The gap between modernity's understanding of authority and that of the Christian is wider than this volume has hitherto acknowledged. We have hitherto talked as if the human search for knowledge was a disinterested search. At one level one would have to say that the human search for truth is something perfectly natural, something we share with other animals. Animals need to explore their environment in order to discover where safety lies and where food can be found. The natural human curiosity that drives us to try to find out what the world is really like is continuous with this. But

if, as the Christian tradition affirms, human beings differ from other animals in being so made
in the image of God that they can find fulfillment only in the worship and love of God, then
the search for a kind of knowledge of God that is
not dependent on the grace of God is doomed to
fail. The human situation will be radically mis-
understood unless we take account of what is
told in the Christian tradition about the Fall.
God's original purpose for human life is that it
should be lived in faith, faith in the goodness of
God. It was God's intention that we should know
only good. The root of all the corruption that has
stained our story was and is the determination to
see for ourselves both good and evil and to ar-
rogate to ourselves a position that we can never
hold — namely, as impartial arbitrators between
good and evil. Because we seek to hold this position yet can never hold it, we are shadowed by
anxiety. We seek for assured knowledge, but the
search does not have the innocence of the natural curiosity of the animal. We seek a security
for ourselves that we were not meant to have, because the only security for which we were made is
security in God, security in God's free grace. The
search for certainty apart from grace has led, as
we have seen, to a profound loss of nerve, a deep

skepticism about the possibility of knowing the truth. We are left shut up in ourselves.

If this is the human situation, God's self-revelation can be only an act of redemption and forgiveness. It cannot be merely the communication of true information. And it is this act that creates (a new creation) the possibility of faith. If we are thinking merely of the communication of information between rational human beings, then of course it is true that the listener, the receptor, exercises personal judgment on the matter being communicated. But if it is the act of one against whom I have offended and who takes the initiative to rescue me from my estrangement, then it is the act that creates the possibility of my response. There is, as the New Testament repeatedly affirms, a new creation, and the Author of the new creation is, necessarily, the final authority. To seek elsewhere for grounds upon which the authority of the Redeemer might be validated would be to reject the act of redemption.

It is obvious that to say these things is to provoke the deep hostility of the "modern" mind, but we cannot evade this confrontation. Every attempt to find grounds for accepting the authority of this revelation in something else must

fail. The only way to communicate its authority is by the communication of the gospel itself.
As we have already noted, it was said of Jesus
by those who heard him that he spoke with authority and not as the scribes. The scribes had
authority only insofar as their teaching rested on
the authority of the Torah. Jesus did not rest his
authority there, but in the fact that his words
and works were the words and works of the Father. It is not that the human responsibility for
judging is canceled. Jesus asks his hearers: "Why
do you not judge for yourselves what is right?"
We are not back in a pre-lapsarian innocence.
And yet, "No one comes to me unless the Father
who sent me draws him." Faith in God's self-
revelation is a gift of God, not an achievement
of the autonomous reason and conscience.

By Faith Alone

It is in this context that one can understand
the passion of Barth's attack on natural theology
and that one can appreciate Buckley's judgment
that a fatal step was taken in Christian theology
when "The Philosopher" was called in to under-
write the authority of revelation. If revelation
were essentially the communication of informa-

tion about God, then it would be appropriate to speak of the innate capacities of the human mind and conscience that enable us to grasp the revelation and make it our own. But if revelation is primarily the act of redemption and reconciliation, if we are speaking not just about information but about incarnation and its immeasurable costliness, then such talk is not appropriate. To use Barth's analogy, if I am drowning and a man risks his own life to save me, it may possibly be true that if I had been twice as heavy he could not have lifted me, and in that sense I made some contribution to the rescue, but it would not be appropriate for me to make this claim. And, leaving that argument aside, even if we are thinking only of revelation as the communication of knowledge about God, we have to reject the claim that this knowledge can be given added certitude by the support of natural theology. For, if one thing is obvious, it is that the "god" whose existence natural theology claims to demonstrate is not the God whose character is rendered in the pages of the Bible, not the God and Father of our Lord Jesus Christ, not the blessed Trinity. It is hard to deny that this "god" is a construct of the human mind and that therefore has the essential character of an idol. One has to ask whether idolatry is a step on the way to the worship of the true God, or a threat to it. If our starting point is the kind of reasoning provided by "the Philosopher" or his many successors, it becomes difficult to accept the possibility of a true incarnation and almost impossible to regard the blessed Trinity as anything other than a piece of mystification. If this is so, must we not say that the knowledge of God given through "natural theology" is not merely a partial knowledge but is a distorted and misleading knowledge?

We have to recognize and reject the idea, so widely accepted, that rational thought can provide us with a kind of reliable knowledge that is neutral in respect of religious commitment and therefore capable of providing a secure foundation for a knowledge of God that does not depend on his own acts of revelation and redemption in history. This supposed neutrality is no neutrality at all, for the reason stated above — namely, that all systematic human thought about the totality of our experience has to take as its starting point some belief about what is ultimate and fundamental — matter, spirit, life, reason, or whatever. There is no neutral standpoint.

The temptation of natural theology is very powerful, because it seems to offer a kind of security that does not depend on faith alone. It is quite common to find, even among committed evangelical Christians, a kind of rationalism that claims to possess indubitable certainty. But this is to fall into the enemy's trap. As Michael Polanyi has said, paraphrasing Einstein, only statements that can be doubted make contact with reality. Our knowledge of God is a matter of faith, faith that is a gift of divine grace. We walk by faith, not by sight. We do not possess indubitable knowledge, but we press forward on the path of faith, looking for the day when we will know as now we are known. A natural theology that purports to offer us grounds of assurance more reliable than those given to us in God's own self-revelation in Jesus Christ is no service to faith but a subversion of it.

Two objections are commonly leveled against this position. The first is often presented as the accusation of fideism. Insofar as this term is used with hostile intent, it appears to rest on a theory of knowledge that — in contrast to Augustine — supposes that the invocation of faith as a necessary element in the enterprise of knowing means the exclusion of the intellect. One would not have much difficulty in exposing the error of this supposition. All knowing rests upon faith commitments, and when a natural theology is proposed as the necessary preparation for the understanding of revelation, one has to uncover the (perhaps unexamined) faith commitments that underpin this theology. The criticism is sometimes expressed by using the phrase "a leap of faith," as though a rejection of natural theology left one with no alternative except an irrational leap into the unknown. But that criticism misses the mark. We are speaking not of an irrational leap into the unknown, but of the responsible acceptance of a personal invitation: "Follow me." The act of following is an act of faith, not of rational calculation of the intellectual credentials of the one who calls and of the probable consequences of following. But it is not an irrational act. Rather, one must ask about the credentials of a philosophy that supposes that there are more reliable clues available for understanding the total mystery of human existence in this world than this personal invitation.

The other objection may be stated as follows. If the faith with which the believer follows Jesus is itself the gift of God, is not God arbitrary in his granting of this gift to some and not to others? I think that the response to this must be along the following lines. If those whom God so calls and to whom is given the gift of faith to respond to the call were called in order that they might be simply the beneficiaries of this calling, there would be ground for making accusation of arbitrary action. But if, as the Bible makes clear, those so called are called not for themselves but that they may be the messengers of his calling for others, then the charge does not stand. Second, although we must acknowledge that we are here seeking to probe something beyond our powers, namely, the inner freedom of God himself to call whom he will, nevertheless those who have been made part of the new creation in Christ would never seek to claim any personal credit for their calling or their faith. If I, at least, interrogate my own experience, I can only confess that the ways by which I was brought to faith in Christ are very mysterious and beyond my own capacity fully to understand. I can only say that it was the immeasurable grace of God. It is true that there is a personal decision — or series of decisions — involved. But these pale into insignificance in comparison with the vast and immeasurable grace of God.

After all this has been said about the enterprise that is called natural theology, something positive must also be said. The territory that natural theology explores may quite properly be explored in the reverse direction. That is to say, it is both possible and necessary, starting from the revelation in Jesus Christ, to explore all its implications in the realm of philosophy. Indeed, this is often a very necessary part of the task of Christian witness. Any mind that has been shaped by modernity will be fully furnished with beliefs and assumptions that seem to make Christian faith untenable or at least very questionable. It is part of the business of Christian testimony to uncover the hidden assumptions that lie behind these beliefs and to show how God's action in Christ in redeeming and revealing opened the way for a truer understanding of the things that had been seen as calling it in question. This kind of activity can have a very important role in helping others on the journey of faith. In that sense they may form part of the pathway to faith. But one must make a distinction between the ways by which people are drawn to faith (which are as various as are the varieties of human nature and experience) and the foundation on which faith rests. This foundation cannot be anything provided by the philosopher. It can only be the action of God himself. The only ultimate authority in the new creation is its Author. We come back to the sentence quoted earlier about Jesus: "He spoke with authority, and not as the scribes." The question that now has to be addressed is: How is this authority mediated to us now two millennia after his incarnate life? That is the question to which we must devote the second section of this volume.

2

The Mediation of Divine Authority

One must approach this question, I think, by asking first about the intention of Jesus. What, according to the record, was Jesus' intention for the future of that work for which he was sent into the world by the Father? We are familiar, of course, with the view that Jesus had no intention for the future because he expected the immediate end of the present age. On this view the long centuries of Christian belief and practice, based on this wrong assumption of Jesus, have been misguided. This has become so widely accepted, even among Christian scholars, that it is necessary to say a few words about it before proceeding. The substantial evidence for Jesus' intention for the future of his community will be indicated below, but two immediate points can be made with reference to the scholarly view that Jesus was mistaken about the central message of the coming reign of God. The first is that this view rests upon a selection of Jesus' sayings that speak of immediacy but ignore the many other sayings that speak of long patience. This is an example of something often found among scholars — a one-dimensional mind that cannot cope with the necessary tensions that are involved in a mature understanding of the human situation. Taken as a whole, the teaching of Jesus about the imminence of the new age calls for a combination of alertness with patience, which is the mark of a good watchman. How else can this be communicated except by sayings and parables that stress one side or the other of the tension? If patience is taken alone, it can lead to drowsiness and sloth; if immediacy alone is stressed, it can lead to a kind of excitement that neglects the ordinary duties of the moment. Christian history is replete with examples of both. The temptation of the great historic churches is to ignore the notes of immediacy and to settle down to a long-term acceptance of things as they are. The temptation of those on the margins of society and of the church is to undervalue long-term perspectives and to live in a state of irresponsible excitement. Both poles of Jesus' teaching have to be held in tension.

The second preliminary point that might be made about the reigning scholarly consensus is this. Many New Testament scholars are eager to emphasize the fact that what we have in the Gospel record is the mind of the early church and not necessarily the *ipsissima verba* of Jesus. Of course this is true: we have what the early church remembered of Jesus, not a tape recording of his words. But if the early writers were as free from dependence upon the exact words of Jesus as this view supposes, is it not odd that they should have recorded sayings that — on this view — had already been amply proved to be mistaken? Is it possible that these early disciples understood the intention of Jesus better than some contemporary scholars? It is a daring thought!

What, then, are we to say about the intention of Jesus concerning the mediation of his authority to future generations? Clearly we have to make one negative statement at the outset: Jesus did not write a book. He chose, called, and prepared a company of people; he entrusted to them his teaching; and he promised them the gift of the Spirit of God to guide them in matters that were beyond their present horizons. Let us look briefly at these three indications of his intention.

1. He formed a community and bound it closely to himself. It is hardly necessary to elaborate this point, for it is the central theme of the four Gospels. But one point seems to me to be of decisive significance. The action of Jesus on the eve of his passion is surely the clearest and most unambiguous evidence of his intention. He was about to be taken from his friends in a shameful death. They would all leave him and flee, for they did not understand his mission. In the few remaining hours before his arrest and death, he acted and spoke in such a way that there could be no possible doubt that he intended them to remain a community committed to him beyond his death. "This is my body given for you; eat it. This is my blood shed for you; drink it." They did not understand, but they obeyed, and in obeying they came to know who he was. Nothing could more clearly and unambiguously reveal his intention that there should be a community continuing his life beyond his death, a continuing life together in this world, not just in the age to come.

2. Jesus taught. Once again, modern scholarship has been skeptical about the extent to which the teachings that are preserved for us in the Gospels can be regarded as the authentic teachings of Jesus. What is available for us,

it is said, is the spiritual experience of the early church, and the teaching of Jesus can be perceived only dimly — if at all — through this veil. This kind of skepticism, if applied to all ancient history, would render it inaccessible. "Methodological doubt" is one of the principles listed by Ernst Troeltsch in his account of the "historical-critical" method of biblical interpretation. It is the application to this particular realm of knowledge of the Cartesian demand for indubitable certainty, a demand that has led to the abandonment of all hope of knowing reality. There is no reason to accept this demand and every reason for treating it with skepticism. It is grounded, of course, in prior beliefs about what is the case. It is true that the sayings of Jesus have come to us in variant forms, but the variations are not such as to leave us in the dark about their substance. Much of this scholarly skepticism is grounded in the experience of those who have never known any culture but a literate one. Those who are familiar with cultures that do not rely on the written word know how tenaciously oral teaching is treasured, preserved, and handed on. (See, e.g., the work of Kenneth Bailey [1992], based on his long residence in the Middle East.) The teachings of Jesus, mediated to us in variant forms by the New Testament writers, have certainly been sharp and clear enough to challenge, disturb, and sustain men and women through sixty generations in both literate and oral cultures.

3. Jesus promised the gift of the Holy Spirit to lead them into the fullness of the truth, a fullness that was beyond their immediate possibility as a group of men and women shaped and limited by a particular culture at a particular moment in its history. Within the pages of the New Testament we can see this promise being fulfilled, as the first apostles combine faithfulness to the teaching of Jesus with freedom and boldness in making new decisions in new situations, relying on the promised guidance of the Spirit.

At the risk of becoming merely speculative, it is worth pausing for a moment at this point to ask whether there is any other way in which divine authority could be mediated to human beings. There would seem to be only two possibilities. One would be that God should make his authority known directly to every individual conscience without intervention of any other human agency. But this suggestion is absurd, for no human being develops either reason or conscience except through participating in the intercourse of a human community, family, society, culture. Because no human experience is totally private, divine revelation could not be totally private. The other possibility is that divine revelation should be a matter of public history. In that case it can be only in events that are limited to a particular time, place, culture. But the whole ongoing course of human history cannot be frozen forever at a particular point. Revelation takes place only if (as has been argued above) it is internalized, made part of a living human consciousness that must necessarily be the consciousness of a human being living in a particular time, place, and culture. It is therefore hard to imagine how there could be any other divine revelation authoritative for the whole of human history except one that embraced the three elements we have noted above: a living community, a tradition of teaching, and the continuing work of the divine Spirit illuminating the tradition in each new generation and each new situation, so that it becomes the living speech of God for that time, place, and culture.

With these preliminary, and perhaps too speculative, observations, I come to the contemporary debate among Christians about authority. Four words are habitually used in this debate. We speak of the authority of Scripture, of the church and its tradition, of reason, and of experience. I propose to look at these four words in that order.

Scripture

It is notorious that Christians are deeply divided on the question of the authority of Scripture. For many centuries the Bible — *the* book — had a place apart from all other literature. It had an authority that was generally unquestioned. It provided the framework for the study of history and the natural world, as well as for the understanding of human life. In the course of the last three centuries, it has been subjected to critical analysis with the tools of modern scientific method. The result is the split with which we are familiar between those who want to affirm biblical authority by defending the factual accuracy of everything that it contains, and those who see the biblical material as an expression of human religious experience, and there are — of course — many other varieties of religious experience. In this situation it has become difficult or impossible to speak with intellectual coherence about the authority of Scripture vis-à-vis any particular aspect of our culture.

What is not often noticed is that this split is

only one manifestation of a much deeper fissure in the culture of modernity as a whole. It might be described briefly as a breakdown of the unity between the subjective and the objective poles of human knowing. It is customary to trace this breakdown back to Descartes, with his search for indubitable knowledge expressed in forms having the clarity and exactitude of mathematics. For the centuries since then, we have been dominated by the ideal of a kind of knowledge that is objective in the sense that it involves no personal commitment on the part of the knower. It is "factual," disinfected of all that personal interest might introduce. What is claimed to be knowledge but cannot be expressed in such "objective" terms is a matter of personal opinion. It is belief rather than knowledge, and — as Locke has taught us — belief is what we fall back upon when knowledge is not available. "Values" — in this view — are matters of personal choice; "facts" are not. No logical ties can bind the two together. Values cannot be derived from facts. The split is visible for all to see in the separation between science and "the humanities" in the curricula of the universities.

Given this situation, it is natural that the Bible has to be understood as belonging to one or other of these two halves of our culture. On the one hand are those who can affirm the authority of Scripture only by regarding it as a collection of factually true statements. On the other are those who see it as material that expresses in symbolic and poetic form certain values including various kinds of religious experience. If the first choice is made, one is on a collision course with the findings of science — in spite of the efforts of the "creationists." If the second choice is made, the Bible simply has to take its place among the many varieties of moral and religious experience. It is part of the history of religions. George Lindbeck (1984) in *The Nature of Doctrine* proposes as an alternative to these two views what he calls a "cultural-linguistic" model for the understanding of Scripture. I find this helpful, but I think that it needs to be related explicitly to the deeper epistemological split of which the fundamentalist-liberal split is a surface manifestation.

In his exposition of the "cultural-linguistic" model for understanding doctrine, Lindbeck uses such phrases as "myths or narratives ... which structure human experience and understanding of self and world ... an idiom that makes possible the description of realities ... something like a Kantian *a priori*" (:32–33). Doctrine, in other words, is not so much something that we look *at* as something that we look *through* in order to understand the world. Here we are raising the epistemological question. All knowing involves a knowing subject, and knowing is only a possibility for a subject who has been inducted into a tradition of knowing embodied in language, symbol, story. Most of what we know is normally not the object of our attention. It is the framework by means of which we order our experience and make sense of it. It is, in Polanyi's phrase, the tacit component in all knowing. When Lindbeck uses the term "cultural-linguistic" to describe his model for doctrine, he is rightly drawing attention to the fact that knowledge requires the ability to use a language and an accepted framework of understanding about "how things are and how things behave" that enables us to make sense of experience. When we use language to communicate information or to share a vision, we do not attend to the words we are using; we attend *through* the words *to* the matter in hand. Only when the words fail to achieve communication do we attend to the words in order to find better ones. And words are part of a culture, of a whole way of understanding and coping with the world that has been developed in a specific community over a period of time. But this necessary subjective component in all knowing does not mean that it is robbed of its objective reference. It is saved from a false subjectivity by being published, made the object of public scrutiny and discussion, tested against new situations. Yet this scrutiny can be undertaken only by knowing subjects who are themselves depending on a culturally shaped tradition.

We seem to be nearing the end of a period in which it was believed that modern science could provide a corpus of universal truth that would be the possession of all human beings, whatever their cultural differences. The enormous impact of Newton's physics has lasted until the present day, with its vision of a self-contained cosmos of particles of matter moving according to precisely determined mathematical laws, a world in which the human mind has no place. The human mind is reduced to a sort of disembodied eye looking at the cosmos from outside, rather than an embodied reality participating in the life of the cosmos, not only as an observer but as an actor who must make personal and risky commitments in order to know anything at all. Paradoxically, this dehumanized model had enormous human appeal. It gave birth to the idea of a universal reason equally applicable in all human cultures and of the universal rights of man simply as man and apart from the accidents of a particular society. But for Lessing it created the "wide ugly ditch" between the universal truths of reason and the accidental happenings of history, and it provoked — most notably in Germany — the reaction in favor of the *Volksgeist* as the bearer of truth. In spite of all that has happened in the recent developments of physics to call into question the Newtonian vision, we are still left with the "two cultures": a culture of science that is supposed to be universally valid for all peoples, and a multiculturalism that brands as imperialistic any claim to discriminate between less and more valuable elements in culture — including the area of religious belief (see Finkielkraut [1988] for a defense of the Enlightenment).

It is simply impossible to remain content with this bisection of human experience into two halves that have no rational connection with each other; therefore, it is impossible to accept the terms of the fundamentalist-liberal debate about the authority of Scripture. Scripture, I suggest, functions (in Lindbeck's phrase) as the cultural-linguistic framework within which the Christian

life is lived and Christian doctrine developed.
The Bible is, to paraphrase Lindbeck, a narrative
that structures human experience and understanding. However varied may be its texture, it
is essentially a story that claims to be *the* story,
the true story both of the cosmos and of human
life within the cosmos. After one has done all
the work that can be done and has to be done to
analyze its structures and trace the origins of its
different parts, it is in its total canonical structure a story that finds the clue to the meaning of
cosmic and human history in the story of a particular people and of a particular man among that
people. Like every telling of the human story, it
is a selection of a minute fraction of the available
records and memories, on the basis of a particular belief about the meaning of the story. World
history as it is normally taught in schools is the
history of the development of civilization. This
might be described as the "natural" way to tell the
story. It places us, the tellers, at the center of the
story. Civilization is defined by our contemporary achievements. We are the civilized people.
History finds its clue in us. History as the Bible
tells it radically subverts this "natural" point of
view. History is to be understood as the patient
wrestling of God with a stupid, deluded, and re-

bellious people — stupid and rebellious precisely because they insist on seeing themselves as the center of the story. The Christian message, as it was first announced by the apostle Paul and others in the synagogues of the ancient world, is that the real point of the story has been disclosed in the events of the cross and resurrection of Jesus. The death of Jesus is the final and conclusive manifestation of the fact that the human race has turned its back upon its Creator; it is as Jesus said, the judgment of this world (John 12:31). And in raising the crucified Jesus from the dead, God the Father has inaugurated a new creation, a new era in which this alienated and rebellious world is given the possibility of a new being in love and obedience to the Creator.

At this point two important points must be made to avoid misunderstanding. The first is this. When we speak of finding in Jesus the clue to the meaning of the whole human story, we are not speaking of a mere cognitive exercise. We are speaking of that act of atonement wrought in Jesus through which we are brought into a loving obedience to the will of God as it is exercised through all human and cosmic history. It is not merely a matter of illumination, of new understanding; it is a matter of reconciliation, of

rescue from alienation, of obedient response to
the divine initiative of love. It is illumination and
new understanding only because it is first a divine action of reconciliation through which we
are brought to that state in which we can say
and know that God works all things together for
good to those who love him. It is only through
this act of atonement that Jesus becomes for us
the clue to history.

The second point to be made is this. When the
word *narrative* is used in theological discourse, it
is sometimes with the implication that the historical truth of the narrative is not important.
The narrative that structures our understanding
of things might be nothing more than a story
told by us to explain our experience, something
with no ontological status beyond our own imag-
ination. It is of the essence of the Christian
faith that this story is the true story. How do
we understand the meaning of "true" in this context? If we follow the lead of the Bible itself, in
its canonical form, it is clear that it contains accounts of happenings and of sayings that are, in
varying degrees, discrepant. The crucial example,
as we have already noted, is the existence of discrepancies in the accounts given of the ministry
of Jesus in the four Gospels. Yet it seems obvious

to any reader who stands within the same faith community as the apostolic writers that these are varying accounts of the same events and sayings. They are different human perceptions of the things that really happened. They share the character of all historical writing. Clearly, however, the Bible also deals with things that cannot be called history in this sense. Neither the creation of the world nor its ending is known to us through contemporary records. What the Bible has to tell us on these is imaginative interpretation arising from the fundamental truth about the human situation that is made known to us and believable by us through God's own redeeming acts. Modern critical scholarship has enabled us to distinguish the many different strands that have been woven together to form the books of the Pentateuch and the historical writings, and to identify the different (and conflicting) interests that are at work — kingship, priesthood, the temple, the land, for example. Beside these wide differences there is the corpus of writings collectively designated as "wisdom literature," with its quite distinct character. (But all of it is held under the oft-repeated reminder that it is fear of the Lord that is the beginning of wisdom.) What is significant is that the New Testament writers can make use of the texts from all these differing elements in the tradition to illuminate the things said about Jesus. The true key to its great variety, the true guide through the debate that continues within the Christian tradition, is to be found in the events concerning Jesus.

The question "Which is the real story?" must determine everything else in our understanding of what it is to be human and what it is to handle rightly the natural world within which human life is set. The Bible, I suggest, functions properly in the life of the church when it functions in the way Lindbeck's language suggests. It functions as the true story of which our story is a part, and therefore we do not so much look *at* it as *through* it in order to understand and deal with the real world. Reverting to Polanyi's language, the Bible ought to function primarily as the *tacit* component in our endeavor to understand and deal with the world. We have to *indwell* the story, as we indwell the language we use and the culture of which we are a part. But because we also live within this other culture, there is necessarily an internal dialogue within us. By all our cultural formation from infancy onward, we are made part of the story of our nation and our civilization. There is something to be learned here from the experience of a foreign missionary. As one learns to enter deeply into the mental world of another people, into their story, as one is drawn by the coherence and rationality of that other story, there is set up an internal dialogue as the precondition for true interpersonal dialogue. But clearly the story functions effectively in providing the structure of understanding only insofar as one really lives the story. The Bible cannot function with any authority except through the lives of those whose story it is, those who "indwell" the story. We cannot speak of biblical authority without speaking of tradition.

Tradition

It is of crucial importance in any discussion of authority to consider the significance of the fact that Jesus did not write a book. The only example recorded of Jesus' writing is when he wrote in the dust. He did not bequeath a book to his followers. He devoted his ministry, as far as we know, to the formation of a community that would represent him to those who would come after. He taught them in ways that would be remembered and passed on to others, but he did not provide a written text. It is, surely, very important that almost all the words of Jesus have come to us in versions that are not identical. To wish that it were otherwise would evidently go against the intention of Jesus. The fact that we have four Gospels rather than one is cited by Muslims as evidence that the real gospel (Injil) has been lost. But the church refused to substitute one harmonized version for the four disparate ones. On the one hand, the New Testament writers insist that what they teach (unless otherwise stated, e.g., 1 Corinthians 7) is a faithful rendering of the intention of Jesus. They are not originators but messengers. But, on the other hand, the teaching of Jesus and the stories of his ministry are told in words shaped to meet different situations.

The story the Bible tells is tied to particular times, places, languages, and cultures. If it were not, it would be no part of human history. It is told as the clue to the entire story — human and cosmic, — from creation to the end of time. It cannot function as the clue to the whole story if it is simply repeated in the same words. It has to be translated, and translation is (fallible) interpretation. The many-layered material of the Old Testament is witness to the repeated retelling of the fundamental story in new terms for new occasions. Jesus expressly tells his disciples, in the Johannine interpretation, that although they have received a true and full revelation of the Father, they have yet much to learn that they cannot learn until later. They are promised that the Holy Spirit will guide them "into all the truth." In view of the perennial temptation to identify the Holy Spirit with the *Zeitgeist*, it is important to note that the promise is that the Spirit will glorify Jesus, for the Spirit will show the church how all things in the cosmos belong to him. Raymond Brown (1966:2:716) paraphrases the promise as "interpreting in relation to each coming generation the contemporary significance of what Jesus has said and done." The church is not tied to a text in such a way that nothing will ever be done for the first time. In new situations, those who "indwell" the story of which Jesus is the center will have to make new and risky decisions about what faithfulness to the Author of the story requires. There can be no drawing of a straight line from a text of Scripture to a contemporary ethical decision; there will always be the requirement of a fresh decision in responsibility to the one whose story it is.

There can therefore be no appeal to Scripture that ignores the continuing tradition of Christian discipleship. That would be to detach Scripture from the story to which it is the clue. But it is a delicate matter to state exactly what is the relation between Scripture and tradition. The tendency of Protestants to isolate the Scriptures from the tradition is, of course, mistaken, for no one has access to a Bible unless someone hands it over (*traditio*). But it is understandable in view of the long experience of the Roman Catholic tendency to treat Scripture and tradition as though they were separate and parallel sources of authority. It is well known that the first draft of the Vatican II document on revelation was entitled "The Two Sources of Revelation." This was rejected, and the final text, simply entitled "Divine Revelation," begins with two chapters on "Revelation Itself" and "The Transmission of Divine Revelation." The first, beginning from God's word incarnate in Jesus Christ, affirms that God "can be known with certainty from the created world, and by the natural light of human reason" (Flannery, 752) and that he has spoken through the prophets and, last of all, in his Son. The second chapter speaks of Christ's commission to the apostles to preach the gospel to all, and of bishops as the successors of the apostles to whom this responsibility to transmit the gospel was entrusted. This tradition "makes progress in the Church, with the help of the Holy Spirit" so that "the Church constantly moves forward towards the fullness of divine truth," (:754). It therefore follows that "both Scripture and Tradition must be accepted and honored with equal feelings of devotion and reverence" (:755).

How is one to state the relation of tradition to Scripture? On the one hand the New Testament is itself part of the tradition. It is obviously based upon oral testimony given at different times under different circumstances. But it claims to be authentic representation of that of which it speaks. "I delivered to you...what I also received," says the apostle (1 Cor. 15:3). On the other hand, the closing of the canon of Scripture implies that what is included in the canon has a higher authority than that which is excluded. What is included has a normative role in relation to all further tradition. In this respect the language of Vatican II is surely too triumphalist. Not all of what has been handed on is to be accepted. The accusation that Jesus leveled against religious teachers of his time (Matt. 15:7ff), that they had made void the word of God by their traditions, has to be leveled against some forms of the Christian tradition. Development in Christian teaching is not a process that has its norm immanent in itself. The promise of Jesus to his disciples that the Holy Spirit would lead them into the fullness of the truth is linked to the promise that, in doing so, the Spirit will glorify Jesus. What the Spirit will show to the church is what belongs to Jesus, and every alleged teaching of the Spirit has to be tested by that criterion (John 16:14f). On the other hand, if it is true that the authority of Scripture lies in the fact that it renders in narrative form the character of the One who is the Author of history and that it is therefore the clue to all history, it seems clear that we cannot follow this clue without taking account of the way that it has been followed in the past. The centuries that have followed the incarnation of the Word have filled out with further content the universal and cosmic implication of the Incarnation, but all that has followed has to be judged by the criteria furnished by the events of the Incarnation. The relation between Scripture and tradition is thus reciprocal, but Scripture is normative in relation to tradition. It is true that it often happens that someone who knows nothing of Jesus or of Christianity reads a Gospel for the first time and is captured by the sheer power of what is read so that he or she turns to Christ in full submission. But it is also true that such a reader will not learn what submission to Christ means except in the fellowship of the church. The book is the book of the community, and the community is the community of the story that the book tells. Neither can be understood without the other.

Tradition, therefore, is not a source of authority separate from Scripture. Rather, it is only by "indwelling" the Scripture that one remains faithful to the tradition. By this indwelling (abiding) we take our place and play our part in the story that is the true story of the whole human race and of the cosmos. By reading the Scriptures as our own story in a shared discipleship with all those — past and present — who acknowledge with us that this *is* the true story, we trust the promise that the Holy Spirit will lead us into the fullness of the truth. Neither Scripture nor tradition furnishes us with an authority that releases us from the risky business of making our own decisions in every new situation. But we have the confidence that, though we may make mistaken decisions, the community that lives by the true story will not be finally lost (Matt. 16:18).

Reason

There is a long tradition that speaks of Scripture, tradition, and reason as the threefold source of authority in regard to Christian doctrine. I have argued that it is a mistake to put tradition alongside of Scripture as though it were a separate and parallel source of authority. The fact that this is a mistake is now widely accepted. It would be equally mistaken to think of reason as a separate and parallel source of authority. No one grasps or makes sense of anything in the Scriptures or in the tradition of scriptural interpretation except by the use of reason. And reason does not operate except within a continuous tradition of speech that is the speech of a community whose language embodies a shared way of understanding. Reason is a faculty with which we try to grasp the different elements in our experience in an orderly way, so that — as we say — "they make sense." It is not a separate source of information about what is the case. It can only function within a continuous linguistic and cultural tradition. We learn to reason as we learn, in childhood, to use words and concepts, those words and concepts that embody the way in which our society makes sense of the world. All rationality is socially and culturally embodied.

When we look back on the "Age of Reason," and especially at the arguments used since the eighteenth century to defend the "reasonableness" of Christianity, it is obvious that the word "reason" was used to denote conformity with a set of assumptions derived from the science and philosophy of the time. The sociologists of knowledge have taught us to use the term "plausibility structure" to denote the structure of beliefs and practices that, in any given society, determine what beliefs are plausible within that society. When reason is adduced as a third source of authority alongside of Scripture and tradition, must we not suspect that what is being appealed to is simply the contemporary plausibility structure? This becomes especially obvious when we look at the "self-evident truths" of which the eighteenth century thinkers spoke. It is obvious to us now that these truths are not self-evident. They are the product of a specific tradition of rationality. There is a parallel here with mathematics. The mathematician John Puddefoot (1987:16) has written: "An axiom is not the foundation of a system, but the product of generations of mathematical enquiry as it has eventually been formalized or axiomatized." Reason operates within a specific tradition of rational discourse, a tradition that is carried by a specific human community. There is no supracultural "reason" that can stand in judgment over all particular human traditions of rationality. All reason operates within a total worldview that is embodied in the language, the concepts, and the models that are the means by which those who share them can reason together. Christian doctrine is a form of rational discourse that has been developed in the community that finds the clue to the rationality of the cosmos as a whole in those events that form the substance of the biblical narrative and in the subsequent experience of those who have done the same. The fact that it is thus rooted in one strand of the whole human story in no way invalidates its claim to universal relevance. It shares this character with every other form of rationality.

Does this formulation lead to a total relativism? No, because all human reasoning is subject to the test of adequacy. There are more and less adequate ways of making sense of human experience and of coping with the world in the light of what sense one can make of it. All forms of rationality are subject to this test. They

are therefore, in vigorous societies, always being modified to take account of new experience.
Sometimes the modifications are minor; sometimes they are cataclysmic. There is a parallel
here with Thomas Kuhn's distinction between
"normal" science and the experience of "paradigm shifts." A way of seeing things is proposed
that "makes sense" in a more adequate way than
the one previously accepted. As Kuhn shows,
there is no overarching logical system that can
justify the switch from one vision to the other;
it is a kind of conversion to a different way of
seeing things that always needs new language.
The only test is adequacy to the reality that is
to be understood and interpreted. The new paradigm cannot demonstrate its reasonableness on
the terms of the old. But the success of the new
paradigm will depend on the vigor and competence of those who have committed themselves
to work with it. In every culture the Christian vision of how things are calls for a conversion and
for the use of new language — none of which can
be shown to be deducible from the reigning plausibility structure. It will convince people of its
superior rationality in proportion to the intellectual vigor and practical courage with which those
who inhabit the new plausibility structure dem-

onstrate its adequacy to the realities of human existence. This will call for the most vigorous and exacting use of reason. In fact, and this is merely an aside, with the widespread breakdown of confidence in the universal applicability of the "reason" of the eighteenth century and the growth of movements like astrology and the New Age, I suspect that one of the main functions of the church in the twenty-first century will be to defend rationality against the hydra-headed *Volksgeist.*

Having said this, however, it will be obvious that the test of adequacy does not claim to offer the kind of indubitable certainty that the Cartesian program claimed. Final certainty belongs to the day of judgment. Until that day, the Christian is called to walk by faith, a faith that is the gift of the One who has reconciled us to himself through the cross. But, as has already been said, the idea that there is available to human beings a kind of indubitable certainty that is independent of divine grace is an illusion.

There is a more specific way in which reason has been invoked as a source of authority, namely, in contradistinction to revelation. Granted that the reigning traditions of rationality in our culture are rooted in the specific history

of Europe, these traditions rest upon the discoveries of the great scientists and philosophers
and historians — discoveries that can be appro-
priated by any student who is willing to make
the necessary effort. In contrast, the Christian
tradition of rationality rests upon alleged revelations that cannot be experimentally checked but
have to be accepted in faith. It is asked, therefore, whether the idea of revelation is compatible
with the requirements of reason. The answer
must be found by looking at two kinds of normal human experience that Martin Buber made
familiar in his distinction between "I and You"
and "I and it." In the latter situation, the autonomous reason is in full control. I analyze, classify,
dissect. I decide what questions to ask and force
the material to answer my questions. Reason is
at the service of my sovereign will. But in the
other situation, the situation of interpersonal relationships, matters are different. I am not in
full control. I cannot force the other person to
answer the questions I ask. Of course, it is possible to treat the other person as an object in
the "it" world and to use the tools of science including, eventually, the tools of the neurosurgeon
to find out how the brain of the person functions. But none of this gives knowledge of the

other person as person. For that I must surrender control. I must listen and expose myself to question. And it is obvious that in thus surrendering sovereignty and moving to the position of one who is questioned, I have not abandoned the use of reason. I am still a rational person making rational judgments and drawing rational conclusions from data. The difference is in the role that reason is called to play. Reason has become the servant of a listening and trusting openness instead of being the servant of a masterful autonomy.

The question at issue, therefore, is not whether or not reason is employed. It is the question whether the total reality with which as human beings we have to deal is to be understood exclusively as lifeless matter, to be investigated by the autonomous human subject, or whether the total reality with which we have to deal is such that a proper knowing of it has more of the character of that knowing which is the fruit of mature personal relationships. The question is not between reason and revelation; it is a question about what is the case, about what kind of reality it is that we are dealing with. If that reality is such that it is amenable to understanding along the lines that we follow in a personal relationship, then it will be reasonable to believe that a tradition of rational discourse could develop from the particular experiences of those to whom the Author of the universe has spoken and who have been alert and humble enough to listen. To "indwell" such a tradition, to live with this paradigm, to endeavor to show in every new generation its adequacy to human experience, its power to "make sense" of new situations, will be a fully rational enterprise. The proposal to set reason against revelation arises only if one is indwelling another tradition of rationality, one that sees the whole of reality merely as an object for investigation. Within this tradition, of course, religion is one of the matters for investigation. There are "religious experiences." In this tradition one does not say, "God spoke to Moses," but, "Moses had a religious experience." The latter formulation leaves the investigator in charge; the former does not. But the long tradition of rational discourse that has followed from accepting the former as valid is not less rational than that which has been developed from the latter. Reason operating within the Christian (or Judaic or Muslim) tradition is still reason.

Experience

The fourth word often used in discussions about
the authority of the Christian message is "experience." It is a newcomer to theology. Until
at least the beginning of the nineteenth century,
the word had the meaning we now convey by
the word "experiment." Apparently it has become
popular in English theology as a translation of
the German *Erlebnis.* One has to ask why it has
become so popular. Earlier theologians did not
appear to need it. Scientists, at least in the natural sciences, do not seem to need it. Neither
a scientist nor anyone else knows anything except by, in some sense, having an experience —
seeing it, reading it, or hearing it. But when
a new star appears in the telescope of an as-
tronomer, she or he does not describe it as a new
astronomical experience; she or he talks about
the star. Why is it otherwise in theology? Why
say, "Moses had a religious experience," rather
than, "God spoke to Moses"? Obviously, it is
because the existence of God cannot be objec-
tively demonstrated, whereas there is plenty of
evidence to show conclusively that people have
religious experiences, and these can be the object of scientific exploration. I suppose that the

most important factor in bringing this word into the theological debate is the impact of Schleiermacher's monumental effort to make a place for Christian belief among its "cultured despisers" by finding the evidence for God in the "feeling of absolute dependence" that, he held, is common to all. If Christian faith must leave the exploration of nature and history to those who operate on other presuppositions, it is in the world of inward feeling that it must find a habitation. Leaving aside such paranormal religious experiences as are the object of investigation by scientists, a great deal of Christian writing, and singing, is about inward experiences of peace and joy and penitence, rather than about realities outside the self.

In what sense can experience function as a source of authority? For those who have had the kind of definable religious experience that can be dated and described, such experience will seem an adequate basis for belief, even if it is also true that similar experiences may be produced by the use of drugs. But such experiences, it would seem, always have some continuity with what has gone before. They are not totally unrelated to the rest of the person's experience of life. And they can continue to provide authority for believing only insofar as they enable the person to "make sense" of the rest of his or her experience. The great majority of Christians, it would seem, hold the faith on grounds other than religious experience in this narrower sense. They will, for example, continue faithfully to pray in private and worship in public along with others, even though there are long periods in which these exercises produce no vivid experiences such as those associated with the conversion of Paul or Augustine. They believe because they have been brought, perhaps from childhood, into the life of the community that believes the gospel, orders its life by it, and finds in so doing that its truth is confirmed in experience.

All experience is within a framework of interpretation. Even the primary experiences of sight and sound make sense only as the infant learns to relate the lights and noises that impinge on it to a real world that is there to be explored. The Christian gospel provides a framework within which all experience is interpreted in terms of the wise and loving purpose of God. Something that, in another framework, is experienced as disaster may within the framework of Christian faith be interpreted as part of God's loving provision. The crucifixion of Jesus is "folly" in one framework, "the wisdom of God" in another. It would therefore be misleading to treat experience as a distinct source of authority for Christian believing, because the character of our experience is a function of the faith we hold. There is a long tradition of teaching in the church that advises us not to depend too much on special religious experiences (precious and needful as they may be from time to time) but to accept the call to walk by faith, trusting that this is the path that leads to the vision of God of which all religious experience can be only a faint glimpse.

The word *experience* certainly stands for something essential in any understanding of authority. God, according to Scripture, desires that his authority be recognized and accepted in the heart and mind and conscience of every human being. God does not desire the kind of unwilling or uncomprehending submission to authority that is the mark of slavery. The Christian believer willingly and joyfully submits to the authority of the One who, in Paul's words, "loved me and gave himself for me" (Gal. 2:20). But God's authority is mediated through the living memory of a community that continually remembers, rehearses, and relives the story that is the theme of the Scriptures. It is in the church's liturgy that the

Bible story becomes a living tradition remembered again and again and, in the preaching of
the Word, reinterpreted and applied to contemporary discipleship. At the heart of all this is
something that may be called experience, but it
is specifically the experience of the contemporary power of the Holy Spirit of God, who is
the Spirit of Jesus, to bring the atoning work of
Christ home to the heart and conscience of the
worshiping community.

All the four elements we have considered have
their place in our recognition of and submission to the authority of God, but only as they
are inseparably combined. Experience, considered apart from that which is experienced —
namely, the reconciling love of God in Christ —
may be experience of something other than the
one true and living God. Reason, considered as
the possession of an autonomous human mind,
excludes us from a whole range of reality. Tradition, uncontrolled by Scripture, can stray far
from the truth as it is in Jesus. And Scripture,
taken simply as the written letter apart from the
quickening work of the Spirit in the life of the
church, can become an instrument of bondage.
In the end there can be no ultimate authority
except the testimony of the Spirit of God in

the heart and conscience of a man or woman. But the presence of the Spirit is promised to the community that indwells that story of which the incarnation, ministry, death, and resurrection of Jesus is the center.

3

Witnessing to Divine Authority in the Context of Modernity

Modernity's suspicion of divine authority was part of a protest in the name of human freedom. This protest was legitimate. The Christendom synthesis of Christianity with political power had led to a place where the church had become an oppressor of human freedom. Dostoyevsky's Grand Inquisitor is the memorable symbol of a Christianity that had parted company with the freedom Jesus came to bring. The religious wars of the seventeenth century finally discredited this synthesis of Christianity with political power. At the same time, the rise of the new science offered a vision of a new basis for human society. The most powerful symbol of this new possibility was provided by the mathematical physics of Isaac Newton. Here was a model of reality that owed nothing to alleged divine revelation. Newton's cosmology seemed to provide an account of everything from the movements of the planets to the falling of an apple, an account that could be, and was to be, developed to cover wider and wider areas of human experience of the world. It was the product of autonomous human reason working freely on the material available to human observation unfettered by any submission to external authority. The darkness of ignorance, superstition, and religion was being banished; the light had come. As Alexander Pope put it, in famous lines:

Nature and Nature's laws lay hid in night;
God said "Let Newton be!" and all was light.

It seemed to be the dawn of a new day. Light had come into a world long shrouded in the darkness of superstitious religious dogma.

But it was also, in a longer historical perspective, the return to a very ancient view. Europe is, after all, only the western end of Asia, and for the millennia before the coming of the gospel, its thought-world was continuous with that of Asia. To anyone familiar with the Indian scene, it is obvious that classical antiquity belongs to the same world of thought. Both the myths of classical antiquity and its philosophical ideas belong to the same world as those of India. Myths, whether or not they have any basis in historical events, provide the background that enables one to give shape to the chaos of experience. They explain what human life is. They tell us where we come from and where we are going. But the classical world, like that of India, was not content with myths. Whether in India or in Greece, the human mind was drawn to seek for the eternal truths lying behind these timebound stories. Ultimate reality must, it seemed, lie at a depth below the ebb and flow of the restless tides that seem to govern human affairs. Myths might be enough for the majority, but the philosopher must reach beyond them.

Scattered among the cities of the Graeco-Roman world there was a people who did not regard themselves as one among the peoples, but as the unique nation constituted by the mighty acts of the one sovereign God, the Creator and Lord of all. They found the key to all understanding not in a philosophy but in a story. One might call it a myth, for it functioned as a myth, giving shape to the whole of human life. But it was not a myth in the usual sense — a story that begins with the noncommittal words "Once upon a time." It was the narrative of events in history, part of the same narrative that tells of the rise and fall of empires and the doings of such historical characters as Cyrus, Alexander, and Caesar. Although the story is told as part of the human history that pagan writers tell, it is the story told as the history of the actions of the God of Israel, the God of Abraham, Isaac, and Jacob. It is history in the sense that it tells of things that really happened, the same things as those of which pagan historians wrote. But it was told as the narrative of the mighty acts of God.

The Christian message, "the gospel," was the announcement first to the Jews and then to pagans that God had crowned all his mighty acts by a supreme act in which sin and death were disarmed and all the nations were invited to become part of the people of the God of Abraham. This was not the introduction of a new religion; it was the announcement that God's promises to Israel were now fulfilled and all the nations were invited to become the people of the God of Israel. All the nations, in other words, were invited to find the clue to the puzzle of human life not in the eternal truths of the philosophers but in the story told in the Bible.

If we ask why we have become accustomed to speak of Europe as a distinct continent and not, as it is, simply as an extension of Asia, it is because for a thousand years the peoples of Europe were shaped into a distinct society by the fact that this story was the framework in which they found meaning for their lives. It was this story, mediated through the worship of the church — its art, architecture, music, drama, and popular festivals — that shaped a culture distinct from the great cultures of the rest of Asia.

Seen in this longer historical perspective, it is obvious that the Enlightenment was a return to the earlier paradigm. It was, of course, prepared for by the events of previous centuries — the invasion of Aristotelian rationalism mediated through Islamic theology, and the revival of classical thought in the Renaissance; but it was in the mid-eighteenth century that this ancient way of seeing things once again took hold of the European mind. From this "enlightened" point of view, the Bible can no longer function as the reigning paradigm, as the story that gives shape and meaning to all human experience, including the experience of evil, pain, and death. It was to be examined, dissected, and analyzed with the tools that were used for the study of any other collection of ancient literary remains. The story it tells has to be understood in terms of the factors that explain any other events in human history. Insofar as it speaks about "the mighty acts of God," this has to be recognized as mythological language. God does not speak to Moses; Moses has a religious experience. We may be willing to say that "in Jesus we encounter God," but we do not say "in Jesus God has come to save us from sin and death." The "mighty acts of God" are mythological, not history.

Seen from this point of view the Bible can have no authority. There may be passages in the Bible that a modern reader finds moving and inspiring (as there are such passages in many other books), but there is no sense in which the Bible can function as authoritative. It is full of self-contradictions. Any proof-text can always be countered by another that recommends a different course of action. A claim for canonical status for the whole book can, on this view, arise only from the arbitrary decision that one element in the whole is to be seen as the key to interpretation.

Of course, it is true that there are great differences, not to say contradictions, within the Bible. It is hardly necessary to give examples. But here everything depends upon the prior question: How do we conceive the human quest for reliable truth? If our quest is that of Descartes — for a final certitude that admits of no possibility of doubt, for "eternal truths of reason" that are independent of contingent happenings in history — then the Bible is not the place to look. To look for this kind of certitude in the Bible is to impose upon the Bible a concept of truth that is foreign to it and is therefore a misuse of the Bible. If we take the Bible itself as our guide to the question "What is truth?" we will find the answer in a long record of struggle between the patient love and wisdom of God and the stubborn, impatient, idolatrous wills of men and women. The story culminates in the coming of the One who is himself the truth — not a timeless proposition but a living Lord who undertakes to lead us into the fullness of the truth as it is present in him. If we accept the authority of the Bible, then we understand ourselves as being *in via*, not possessors of eternal truth, but part of a living tradition of discipleship, on the way to the truth that will be perfectly known on the day when the Author of the story brings it to its end and consummation. If one approaches the Bible from the point of view of the Enlightenment, looking for "eternal truths of reason" beyond the partial and ever-changing glimpses of truth that human beings have claimed during the long human story, then the Bible will appear to be only a jumble of mutually inconsistent truth-claims. Any claim to have the key to its unity and therefore to its "real" message will appear as arbitrary. It will be the expositor's personal decision based upon prior epistemological commitments. But it will be otherwise if we recognize that the possession of eternal and indubitable "truths of reason" is not something available to human beings still *in via*. There is nothing logically incoherent about recognizing the Bible as embodying the long and patient struggle of the living God to lead a people into the true knowledge of his purpose for the creation, or in believing that the same living God has become part of the story in Jesus Christ, addressing a personal call to men and women to find in following him the way into the fullness of truth. In that case, the great discrepancies within the Bible will not be ground for rejecting its authority. All traditions of understanding live by means of continual debate about their center. Without such debate a tradition of understanding dies.

The Bible is, of course, full of internal tensions. One may cite, for example, the difference between Paul and James on the matter of faith and works; the difference between the sharply contrasted estimates of kingship in chapters 8 and 9 of First Samuel; or the difference between exclusivism in Ezra-Nehemiah and inclusivism in Ruth and Jonah. Perhaps the ultimate tension is between the wrath and love of God, a tension so vividly present within the teaching of Jesus himself. It is because this tension finds its only interpretation and resolution in the atoning death and resurrection of Jesus that we must accept his invitation to take up the cross and follow as the only true hermeneutical key to the Bible as a whole. When this key is accepted, the whole Bible is seen as a unity whose coherence is found in the total fact of Christ. This does not render unnecessary or unimportant the scholarly effort to understand the original intentions of Old Testament writers or the meaning of events as they were understood by those who lived through them. It does not mean, of course, that the ancient prophets knew beforehand the contents of the four Gospels. It does mean, however, that the full significance of these words and events is not understood until it is seen in the light of the events concerning Jesus. The meaning of an event or a word depends upon the framework in which it is placed. The Christian claim, from the first preaching of the apostles and of Jesus himself, is that the true meaning of all that is contained in the Hebrew Scriptures is to be grasped only when they are placed in the total context of the ministry of Jesus.

The centuries since Newton have seen the project of enlightenment carried to the furthest parts of the earth, offering a vision for the whole human race of emancipation, justice, material development and human rights. It was, and is, a noble project. Yet it has failed disastrously to deliver what was promised. Forces of darkness, irrationality, and violence are perhaps more devastating throughout the world today than they have ever been. And in Europe itself, the birthplace of the Enlightenment and long regarded as the secure bastion of its values, there is disintegration. Those who fought to overthrow the dark forces of fascism and national socialism in the Second World War and believed that Europe would never sink again into such barbarism have lived to see these same forces once more taking the stage. Even where such violent forms of irrationality are only on the margins of society, the great visions for the future that inspired the social legislation of the nineteenth and twentieth centuries are now widely rejected. Rational planning for human welfare is widely abandoned in favor of leaving everything to the irrational forces of the market.

It would seem that the splendid ideals of the Enlightenment — freedom, justice, human rights — are not "self-evident truths," as the eighteenth century supposed. They seemed self-evident to a society that had been shaped for more than a thousand years by the biblical account of the human story. When that story fades from corporate memory and is replaced by another story — for example, the story of the struggle for survival in a world whose fundamental law is violence — they cease to be "self-evident." Human reason and conscience, it would seem, do not operate in a vacuum. Their claim to autonomy is unsustainable. They are shaped by factors that are in operation prior to the thinking and experience of the individual. They are shaped most fundamentally by the story that a society tells about itself, the story that shapes the way every individual reason and conscience works.

One way of describing the great shift in European consciousness that took place in the seventeenth and eighteenth centuries is to say that it was a shift in the place where reliable truth was to be found from a story to a set of timeless laws. The cosmos as it is conceived in the Newtonian model has no history. Its laws of mass and momentum operate eternally. This was to become the model for reliable truth, the kind of truth for which the word *science* was now reserved, truth that could in principle be stated in timeless formulae of mathematics. For truth in this sense, accidental happenings in history have, as Lessing said, no relevance. Henceforth, reliable knowledge was to be scientific, and in pursuit of this kind of knowledge faith as alleged revelations has no place. Careful observation and rational ordering of the data are the essential conditions for knowledge. The "scientific method," as classically articulated by Descartes, was to be the pathway to reliable knowledge.

There is one thing, however, that the method of Descartes can never discover — namely, the purpose, if any, for which this whole cosmic mechanism exists. The reason is obvious. A purpose, until it is realized, is hidden in the mind of the one whose purpose it is. When it has been fully realized, the product is available for study by the method of science. Until that time, it is not. The purpose can be known only if the one whose purpose it is chooses to reveal it. *If* purpose is a significant category of explanation, then revelation is an indispensable source of reliable knowledge. It is of the greatest significance for later development that Francis Bacon, at the dawn of the modern scientific movement, retained the concept of causation as a category of explanation but eliminated the concept of purpose. The cause-effect links between different things can be discovered by observation and reasoning, but purpose cannot be so discovered. Yet is it not clear that we have not understood anything fully if we have understood only the chains of causation that are operating and have no clue to the purpose for which the thing exists. The result has been the very odd situation in which millions of "enlightened" products of the scientific method have believed that the cosmos can best be understood as a vast machine that, unlike any machine that has ever existed, was constructed by no one for no purpose. It is difficult to imagine a more self-contradictory and irrational belief.

This picture of our situation has broken down. Although the ideas of modernity still have a strong residual hold at the level of unacknowledged assumptions, for an increasing number of people there is no longer any confidence in the alleged "eternal truths of reason" of which Lessing spoke. Eternal and ultimate truths are unknowable, and any claim to know them is simply an assertion of the will to power. In respect of such claims one does not ask, "Is it true?" but, "In whose interest is the claim being made? What support does it have? Who is hoping to profit by it?"

In this situation it is a very great mistake for Christians to seek to commend the authority of the gospel by asserting what is said to be eternal and indubitable truths. The knowledge of God given to us through the gospel is a matter of faith, not of indubitable certainty. This statement is challenged by some Christians who fear that it opens the door to relativism and subjectivism. But this challenge has to be resisted. It comes from captivity to the typical modernist illusion that there is available to us a kind of objective knowledge wholly sanitized from contamination by any "subjective" elements. There are some conservative Christians who be-

lieve that it is only by asserting the *objective* truth
of the gospel that one can affirm its authority.
The most damaging effect of this is that it severs
the knowledge of God from the grace of God.
As I have already argued, the knowledge of God
can be only by grace through faith. The attempt
to eliminate this deeply personal element in the
knowledge of God, out of fear of subjectivism,
can lead only to a kind of hard rationalism that is
remote from the gospel. Certainly we must insist
on the objectivity of what we affirm in preaching the gospel if that means that we are speaking
of realities "beyond ourselves" and not just of our
own feelings. But God is not an object for our
investigation by scientific methods in the style of
Descartes. God is the supreme Subject who calls
us by grace to put our faith in Him. One may
thus speak of two kinds of certainty. There is the
kind of certainty for which Descartes sought and
that modernity has constantly sought, a certainty
that rests on my own possession of indubitable
truth. And there is the kind of certainty that is
expressed in the apostolic word: "I know whom
I have believed, and I am sure that he is able
to guard until that Day what has been entrusted
to me" (2 Tim. 1:12). Here the certainty rests
not in my own competence as a knower, but in

the faithfulness of One whom I have learned to know, and the knowing is a matter of believing that looks forward to a day when we shall know in full and without possibility of doubt.

Any discussion of biblical authority runs the risk that we may begin with the concept of authority that operates in our culture and then ask whether the Bible has this kind of authority. In a culture that has learned to accept as authoritative only those truth-claims that can be validated by the method of Descartes, it is natural that Christian apologists should fall into this trap, as some conservative Christians have done. Just as when we say, "Jesus is Lord," we must take our definition of lordship from Jesus, thus subverting the reigning concept of lordship in our culture, so when we speak of the Bible as "the word of God" we must learn from the Bible itself what kind of a word God speaks. We must let the Bible speak for itself, opening our minds to be reshaped by this listening. When we do this, we find ourselves drawn into a debate in which reason and conscience are fully engaged. The Bible comes to exercise authority over us as, in company with the believing community and in the communion of the Holy Spirit, we allow ourselves to be drawn, not coerced, into the continuing discussion by which the church is called to maintain the integrity of its witness to the mighty acts of God.

If our model of truth is that suggested by Newton's cosmology — namely, that of timeless realities governed by eternal laws — then belief can be only a preliminary step on the way to knowledge. The aim should be a total knowledge that leaves no room for either faith or doubt. But if our model of truth is embodied in a story, a story of which we are ourselves a part, then the only available form of knowledge is by faith in the One who is the author of the story. We are part of the story, and we have not seen its completion. The most exhaustive examination of things now available for inspection can do no more than furnish grounds for guesswork about the future. The only knowledge we can possibly have of the purpose, and therefore the meaning of this entire cosmic story of which we are a part, is by faith in the One whose purpose it is and who has, by grace to us who had shut ourselves off from this knowledge, called us to be co-workers with him in the fulfillment of this purpose. It follows that the only way in which we can affirm the truth and therefore the authority of the gospel is by preaching it, by telling the story, and by our corporate living of the story in the life and worship of the church. It means that we reject a conception of "objective truth" that seeks it in a series of timeless propositions in the affirmation of which we are not personally involved, for which we do not have to commit our whole lives; it means that we affirm that truth is to be found only in the personal commitment to a life of discipleship with Him who is himself the truth. We have to tell and enact the story.

It need hardly be said that this has immense implications for the way in which we conceive of the task of theology. Theology in the period of modernity has been largely captive to academic institutions that are controlled by the assumptions of modernity. In such institutions it is customary to hear that what is being taught is to be distinguished from what is called "confessional" theology. The implication is that, in contrast to what is done in the church, there is offered here a "scientific" account of the matters with which theology deals. Once again we are dealing with the modern illusion of a kind of objectivity from which the personal commitment of the knowing subject has been eliminated. The temptation for some Christians is simply to stop their ears against this and to develop another kind of objectivity based on a doctrine of scriptural inerrancy. But this is no solution. What has to be done is to affirm the story as the clue to all understanding and to engage the academic world in dialogue that openly challenges the assumptions of modernity.

Perhaps one final point needs to be made. If, in the postmodern world, we tell our story, we will be met with the rejoinder: "Yes of course. That is your story. But there are other stories. Why should we believe this one?" How does the Christian respond to this? Clearly we must resist the temptation to propose some supposedly more fundamental and more reliable truth on the basis of which the story of the gospel could be validated. Certainly we may try to show how the biblical story makes sense of human life in a way that no other can; but even this becomes clear only when one is part of the story. In the end, the only answer we have to give to the question is along such lines as these: "I have been called and commissioned, through no merit of mine, to carry this message, to tell this story, to give this invitation. It is not my story or my invitation. It has no coercive intent. It is an invitation from the one who loved you and gave himself up for you." That invitation will come with winsomeness if it comes from a community in which the grace of the Redeemer is at work. Whether or not it is accepted is not a matter in our power. To be anxious about it, to fret about it, is a sign of unbelief. The one who invites is in control, not we. Kenneth Cragg has said that an anxious witness is a contradiction of terms. We have to tell and live the story faithfully; the rest is in God's hands. What matters is not that I should succeed, but that God should be honored.

References Cited

Bailey, Kenneth E. 1992. *Finding the Lost.* St. Louis: Concordia Publishing House.

Brown, Raymond E. 1966. *The Gospel According to John. Anchor Bible.* Garden City: Doubleday and Co.

Buckley, Michael. 1987. *At the Origins of Modern Atheism.* New Haven: Yale University Press.

Clouser, R. A. 1991. *The Myth of Religious Neutrality.* Notre Dame: Notre Dame University Press.

Finkielkraut, Alain. 1988. *The Undoing of Thought.* Trans. Dennis O'Keeff. London: Claridge Press.

Flannery, Austin, O.P. 1992. *Vatican Council II: The Conciliar and Post Conciliar Documents.* Grand Rapids: Wm. B. Eerdmans Publishing Co. New revised edition.

Lindbeck, George A. 1984. *The Nature of Doctrine.* Philadelphia: Westminster Press.

Polanyi, Michael. 1958. *Personal Knowledge: Towards a Post-Critical Philosophy.* London: Routledge & Kegan Paul.

Puddefoot, John. 1987. *Logic and Affirmation.* Edinburgh: Scottish Academic Press.